T0272931

THE NIKOLA TESLA
ELECTRIFYING
PUZZLE BOOK

THIS IS A CARLTON BOOK

Published in 2019 by
Carlton Books Ltd
20 Mortimer Street
London W1T 3JW

ISBN 978-1-78739-245-8

10 9 8 7 6 5 4 3 2 1

Editorial Director: Chris Mitchell
Design Manager: Stephen Cary
Picture Research: Steve Behan
Production: Jess Arvidsson

The copyright holder would like to thank Corbis, Dover Books, Getty
Images, Istockphoto.com, Mary Evans Picture Library, Shutterstock.com
& Topfoto.co.uk for their kind permission to reproduce the photographs
and illustrations in this book.

Every effort has been made to acknowledge correctly and contact the
source and/or copyright holder of each picture and Carlton Books Lim-
ited apologizes for any unintentional errors or omissions, which will be
corrected in future editions of this book.

Printed in Dubai

Puzzle content previously published in *The Nikola Tesla Puzzle Collection*

THE NIKOLA TESLA
ELECTRIFYING PUZZLE BOOK

PUZZLES INSPIRED BY
THE ENIGMATIC INVENTOR

Tim Dedopulos

CARLTON
BOOKS

CONTENTS

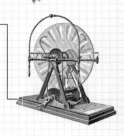

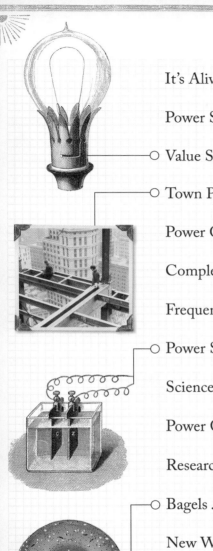

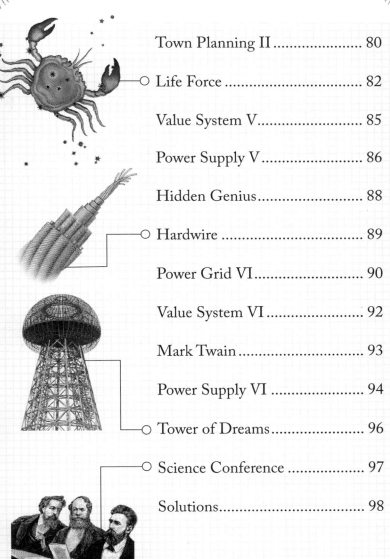

INTRODUCTION

Electrical power is something we now take for granted; with the touch of a button electrons flow and the devices we have come to depend on are brought to life.

But it wasn't until the latter part of the 19th century that an explosion of innovations in electrical engineering and radio wave transmission would lead to our era of worldwide communication. These innovations were pioneered by many great minds, some of whom remain in relative obscurity while others have become household names.

The Alternating Current (AC) that brings light and other essential comforts to our homes owes much to the work of a visionary genius named Nikola Tesla.

Tesla's story is replete with impossible ambition, incredible breakthroughs and no small amount of personal tragedy. Like many talented men who dream of a better tomorrow, he found himself at odds with and exploited by the world of commerce. Tesla's ideas were both ridiculed and appropriated by his rivals, and he died in poverty.

The rivalry between Tesla and Thomas Edison – known as the War of the Currents – has become a topic of much fascination in recent years. Tesla is hailed by

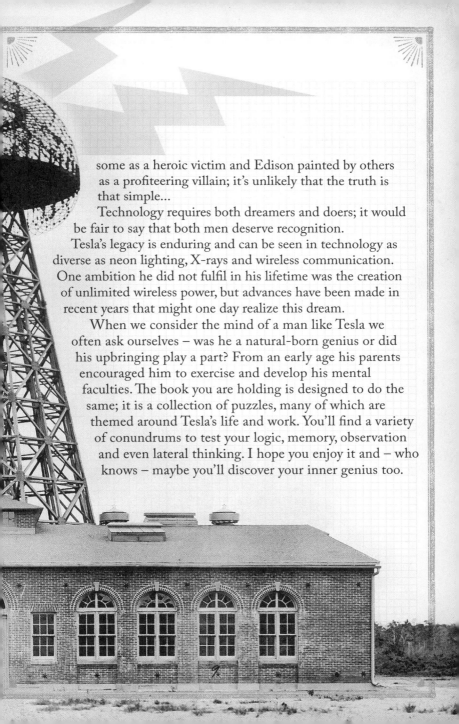

some as a heroic victim and Edison painted by others as a profiteering villain; it's unlikely that the truth is that simple...

Technology requires both dreamers and doers; it would be fair to say that both men deserve recognition.

Tesla's legacy is enduring and can be seen in technology as diverse as neon lighting, X-rays and wireless communication. One ambition he did not fulfil in his lifetime was the creation of unlimited wireless power, but advances have been made in recent years that might one day realize this dream.

When we consider the mind of a man like Tesla we often ask ourselves – was he a natural-born genius or did his upbringing play a part? From an early age his parents encouraged him to exercise and develop his mental faculties. The book you are holding is designed to do the same; it is a collection of puzzles, many of which are themed around Tesla's life and work. You'll find a variety of conundrums to test your logic, memory, observation and even lateral thinking. I hope you enjoy it and – who knows – maybe you'll discover your inner genius too.

9

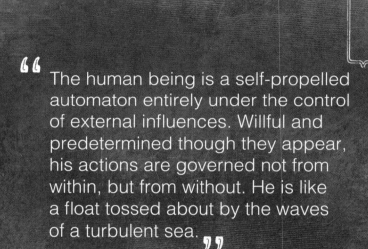

“ The human being is a self-propelled automaton entirely under the control of external influences. Willful and predetermined though they appear, his actions are governed not from within, but from without. He is like a float tossed about by the waves of a turbulent sea. „

NIKOLA TESLA

11

BORN IN
A STORM

Nikola Tesla was born at the stroke of midnight, 10 July 1856, in the village of Smiljan, which lies on the eastern edge of Austria-Hungary (now Croatia).

His mother, Georgina Đuka, was a skilled weaver and a talented inventor in her own right; Milutin, his father, was a priest.

A violent electrical storm raged overhead as Tesla came into the world, an appropriate portent for a child who would become the 'Master of Lightning'.

Let your mind be like lightning now and answer this question quickly:

There are 31 days in July. But how many months have 28 days?

SOLUTION ON PAGE 100

COMPLETE THE GRID I

What should go in the black square to complete the grid?

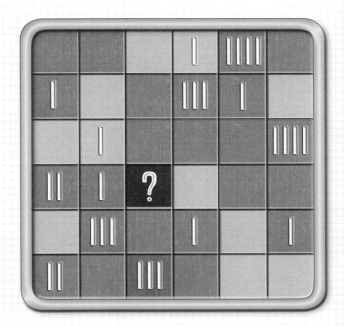

SOLUTION ON PAGE 101

FAITH, HOPE & CLARITY

Milutin Tesla expected his son to join him in the clergy, but Nikola contracted cholera before he could join the seminary. Lying on his sick bed close to death, the young genius begged his father to let him study engineering instead of theology. Milutin agreed, Nikola made a dramatic recovery and his place in history was assured.

On the next page you can see a variety of images. Take a couple of minutes to picture them in your mind and then turn over the page…

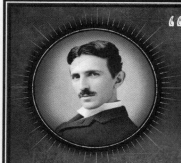

" Let the future tell the truth, and evaluate each one according to his work and accomplishments. The present is theirs; the future, for which I have really worked, is mine. "

NIKOLA TESLA

SOLUTION ON PAGE 102

15

Two of the items above have swapped positions. Can you say which?

SEQUENCE I

Complete the sequence below.

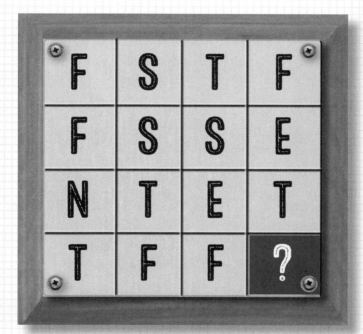

F	S	T	F
F	S	S	E
N	T	E	T
T	F	F	?

SOLUTION ON PAGE 103

STONE AGE PIONEERS

Some of humanity's greatest inventions predate recorded history. Just for fun let's find out who invented what, what inspired their discovery and how they were rewarded by their tribe.

1. *The caveman who was banished from his tribe after eating some strange mushrooms was neither Nigel nor the inventor of fire.*

2. *Stig's invention of the plough was not inspired by a storm and neither was the inventor who was worshipped as a god.*

3. *The inventor of the bow was made chief of his tribe.*

4. *Neither Ugg, nor the inventor of the bow, nor the caveman who went hunting, had a monument built in their honour.*

	Invention	Inspiration	Reward
Zog			
Ugg			
Stig			
Nigel			

	Plough	Fire	Bow	Wheel	Mushrooms	Hunting	Sabre-tooth Tiger	Thunderstorm	Worshipped	Promoted to Chief	Monument	Banished
Zog												
Ugg												
Stig												
Nigel												
Worshipped												
Promoted to Chief												
Monument												
Banished												
Mushrooms												
Hunting												
Sabre-tooth tiger												
Thunderstorm												

SOLUTION ON PAGE 104

POWER GRID I

1. Run a single, unbroken wire around the grid that passes through each of the relays to complete the circuit.

2. The wire must enter and leave each square through the centre of one of its four sides.

3. If the wire enters a black relay, it must immediately turn 90 degrees left or right on that square. It must also pass straight through the square it came from and the square it leads to.

4. If the wire enters a silver relay, it must pass straight through the square. It must also turn left or right in the next and/or preceding square.

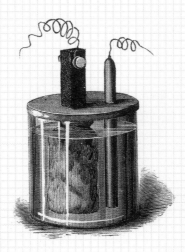

SOLUTION ON PAGE 105

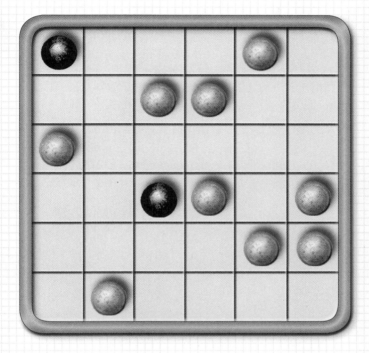

VISIONS

It was clear from an early age that Tesla's mind worked on a different frequency; he was given to vivid waking dreams that he could barely distinguish from reality. His inspiration for hydro-electric power apparently came from a vision of a wheel being turned by the Niagara Falls. In 1896 this dream would become a reality and usher in the Electronic Age.

On the opposite page you can see a variety of images.
Take a couple of minutes to picture them in your mind
and then turn over the page…

" Today's scientists have substituted mathematics for experiments, and they wander off through equation after equation, and eventually build a structure which has no relation to reality. "

NIKOLA TESLA

SOLUTION ON PAGE 106

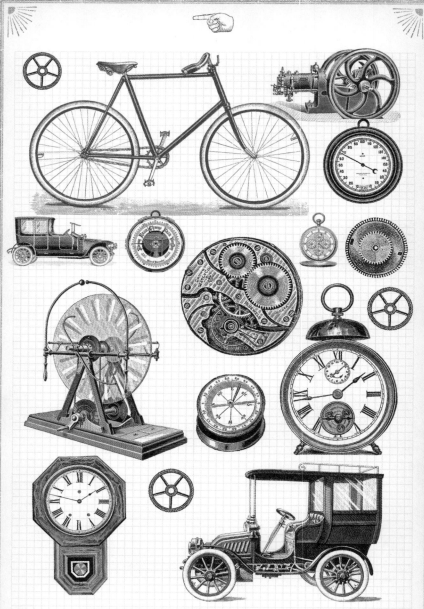

Four of the items above have changed positions. Can you say which?

WATERY GRAVE

The bodies of three men were found in three separate rooms. Each room was full of water and nothing else.

The coroner reported that each of the men died of different causes, but in each case it was as a direct result of being in the water.

Only one of the men drowned. So how did the other two die?

SOLUTION ON PAGE 107

PATTERN
RECOGNITION

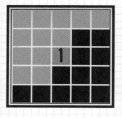
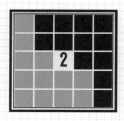
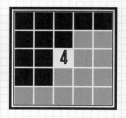

Which of the shapes below completes the sequence?

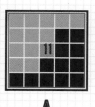

A   **B**   **C**   **D**

COMPLETE THE GRID II

What should go in the black square to complete the grid?

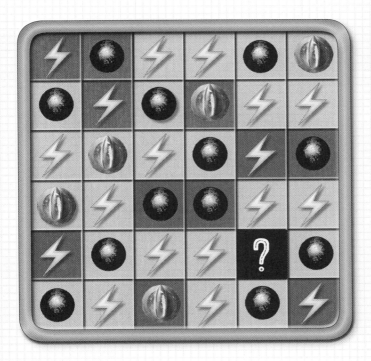

SOLUTION ON PAGE 108

FAMILIARITY

Clara and Betty had come to hear the last will and testament of the late electrical tycoon, Sir Avery Shorte-Fuse.

Just as the proceedings were about to begin, the doors burst open and a young woman entered the room.

Neither Clara nor Betty had ever set eyes on the woman before, yet both angrily exclaimed, "Oh drat, it's Diane!"

Can you explain how they could recognize the stranger and why they would react so negatively?

SOLUTION ON PAGE 108

VALUE SYSTEM I

Work out the value of each component to determine what number replaces the question mark.

SOLUTION ON PAGE 109

IT'S ALIVE!

Using electricity to reanimate dead tissue was once considered a scientific possibility. Four lonely scientists have decided to create "golems" from assorted body parts. Can you say where each professor created his golem, the name he gave it and what happened?

1. Professor Knutz moved to a disreputable neighbourhood in Berlin to conduct his experiments.

2. The whole of New York City suffered a power outage when the golem called "Bob" was brought to life. Unsurprisingly the disgruntled citizens did not make him a national hero.

3. Not all of the golems were monstrous; one professor thought his golem was so lovely, he stayed in Paris and married it.

4. Professor Phreekdoubt suffered an existential crisis after talking to his golem and ended up in therapy; he did not name his creation "Bob."

5. The wealthy professor Bankenstein named his golem "Jerry."

6. The golem called "Ron" was not made in London.

Professor	Location	Golem	Outcome
Van der Volt			
Bankenstein			
Knutz			
Phreekdoubt			

	New York	London	Paris	Berlin	Ron	Phil	Jerry	Bob	Got married	Bloody rampage	Therapy	National hero
Van der Volt												
Bankenstein												
Knutz												
Phreekdoubt												
Got married												
Bloody rampage												
Therapy												
National hero												
Ron												
Phil												
Jerry												
Bob												

SOLUTION ON PAGE 109

POWER SUPPLY I

1. Place a battery (⚡) in a square adjacent to each lightbulb on the grid.

2. Adjacent squares share a side (north, south, east and west) not just a corner.

3. No lightning bolt can be placed adjacent to another battery.

4. The numbers tell you how many batteries must be placed in each row or column.

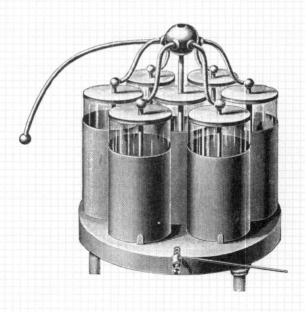

SOLUTION ON PAGE 110

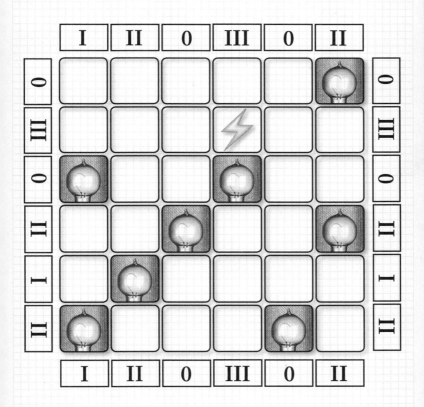

VALUE SYSTEM II

Work out the value of each component to determine what number replaces the question mark.

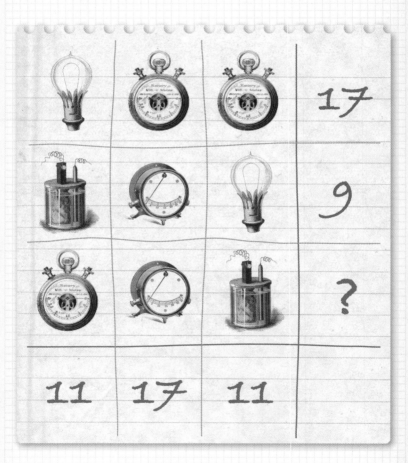

SOLUTION ON PAGE 111

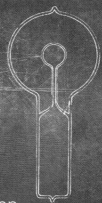

"It seems that I have always been ahead of my time. I had to wait 19 years before Niagara was harnessed by my system, 15 years before the basic inventions for wireless, which I gave to the world in 1893, were applied universally."

NIKOLA TESLA

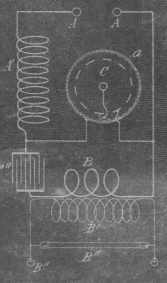

TOWN PLANNING I

Your city is divided into six districts. The mayor has decreed that each district shall have one of each of the following facilities:

You must make sure that there is no more than one of each facility in each column and row, and that no facilities of the same type are adjacent to one another.

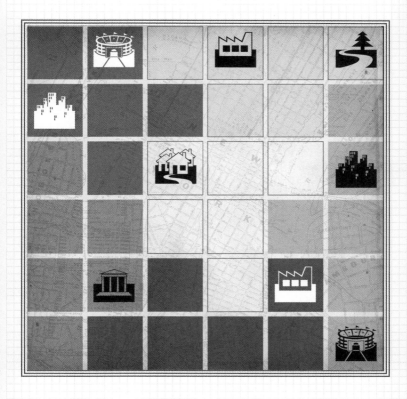

 Housing   Factory   Offices

 School   Stadium   Park

SOLUTION ON PAGE 112

POWER GRID II

1. *Run a single, unbroken wire around the grid that passes through each of the relays to complete the circuit.*

2. *The wire must enter and leave each square through the centre of one of its four sides.*

3. *If the wire enters a black relay, it must immediately turn 90 degrees left or right on that square. It must also pass straight through the square it came from and the square it leads to.*

4. *If the wire enters a silver relay, it must pass straight through the square. It must also turn left or right in the next and/or preceding square.*

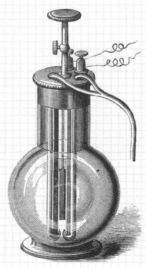

SOLUTION ON PAGE 113

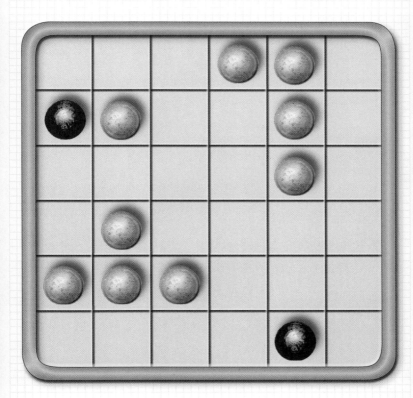

COMPLETE THE
GRID III

What belongs in the empty box?

 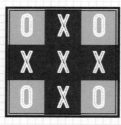 

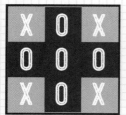 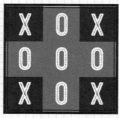 

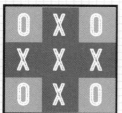 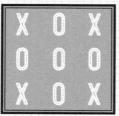

SOLUTION ON PAGE 114

40

FREQUENCY

Can you identify these four pioneers of science and technology just from the frequency of letters in their names?

1

A	B	C	D	E	F	G	H	I	J	K	L	M
2	0	1	0	1	0	0	0	1	0	0	0	0

N	O	P	Q	R	S	T	U	V	W	X	Y	Z
2	1	0	0	0	1	1	0	0	1	0	0	0

2

A	B	C	D	E	F	G	H	I	J	K	L	M
1	1	0	0	3	0	0	0	2	0	0	1	0

N	O	P	Q	R	S	T	U	V	W	X	Y	Z
2	0	0	0	1	1	2	0	0	0	0	0	0

3

A	B	C	D	E	F	G	H	I	J	K	L	M
4	0	1	1	1	1	0	1	1	0	0	1	1

N	O	P	Q	R	S	T	U	V	W	X	Y	Z
0	0	0	0	1	0	0	0	0	0	0	1	0

4

A	B	C	D	E	F	G	H	I	J	K	L	M
2	0	0	0	1	0	0	0	1	0	1	2	0

N	O	P	Q	R	S	T	U	V	W	X	Y	Z
1	1	0	0	0	1	1	0	0	0	0	0	0

SOLUTION ON PAGE 114

POWER SUPPLY II

1. Place a battery (⚡) in a square adjacent to each lightbulb on the grid.

2. Adjacent squares share a side (north, south, east and west) not just a corner.

3. No lightning bolt can be placed adjacent to another battery.

4. The numbers tell you how many batteries must be placed in each row or column.

SOLUTION ON PAGE 115

42

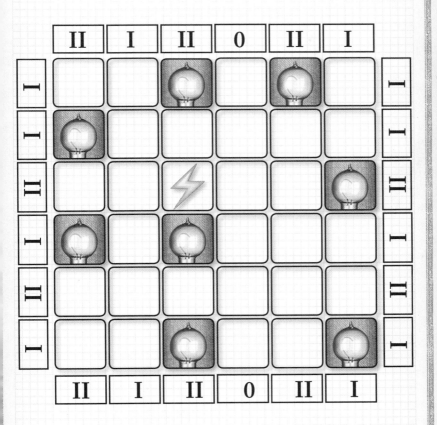

SCIENCE VS CATASTROPHE

Four (quite mad) scientists are working hard to save the world from impending doom.

Can you say which scientist is a specialist in which field, the nature of catastrophe he predicts and what solution he proposes?

1. *Harry Stottle was not the astrophysics professor who proposed building a fleet of spacecraft and moving to Mars to avoid the catastrophe.*

2. *Ty Neilson believed that living underground was our only hope, whereas the professor who predicted an imminent Ice Age thought we could only survive with the help of robot servants.*

3. *Palaeontologist Gary Leo was adamant that the greatest threat did not come from outer space.*

4. *At a press conference the eminent geologist stated, "Our planet is under attack from extra-terrestrial aliens!" Professor Dorkins said, "There is absolutely no danger of a meteor strike."*

5. *The marine biologist did not think accelerated genetic mutation could save us from disaster.*

Professor	Field	Catastrophe	Solution
Dick Dorkins			
Ty Neilson			
Harry Stottle			
Gary Leo			

	Geology	Astrophysics	Palaeontology	Marine Biology	Global flood	Alien invasion	Ice Age	Meteor strike	Genetic mutation	Robot servants	Live underground	Move to Mars
Dick Dorkins												
Ty Neilson												
Harry Stottle												
Gary Leo												
Genetic mutation												
Robot servants												
Live underground												
Move to Mars												
Global flood												
Alien invasion												
Ice Age												
Meteor strike												

SOLUTION ON PAGE 116

POWER GRID III

1. Run a single, unbroken wire around the grid that passes through each of the relays to complete the circuit.

2. The wire must enter and leave each square through the centre of one of its four sides.

3. If the wire enters a black relay, it must immediately turn 90 degrees left or right on that square. It must also pass straight through the square it came from and the square it leads to.

4. If the wire enters a silver relay, it must pass straight through the square. It must also turn left or right in the next and/or preceding square.

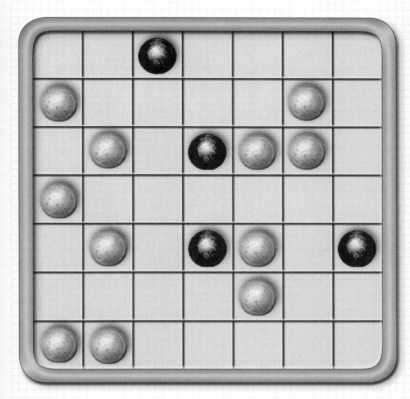

SOLUTION ON PAGE 117

47

RESEARCH

Three types of specialist are working on a project.

The biochemists are always 100% truthful.
The statisticians are always 100% untruthful.
The accountants are able to make whatever they say true.

The director selects 18 researchers and assigns them to three teams of six.

Alpha Team consists of specialists all of the same type.
Bravo Team has an even split of two types of specialist.
Charlie Team has an even split of all three types.

Unfortunately the network crashes on the first day and team details are lost. The director faces three teams but has no way of knowing which team is which.

Team 1 says: "All our members are biochemists."
Team 2 says: "All our members are statisticians."
Team 3 says: "All our members are accountants."

The director decides that she needs to drop the mendacious statisticians. But how many people must she fire?

SOLUTION ON PAGE 118

BAGELS

Each morning the bagel seller buys his bagels at two cents each then sets off to make his deliveries. He arrives at Tesla's lab at midday and sells his last bagel for one dollar fifty.

"You must be making a fortune," remarked Tesla.

"Not even close," said the bagel seller miserably, "you're my one and only customer."

On his way to Tesla's lab the bagel seller must travel through the territories of three notorious street gangs. In each territory he is forced to pay a tariff of half of the bagels he is carrying, plus two more, to the gang leader.

So does the bagel seller make a profit at all?

SOLUTION ON PAGE 119

NEW WORLD

In 1884, after an eventful voyage, Tesla arrived in the United States with just four cents and a letter of recommendation in his pocket. But he had a head full of ideas and a determination to live the American Dream.

On the next page you can see a variety of images. Take a couple of minutes to picture them in your mind and then turn over the page...

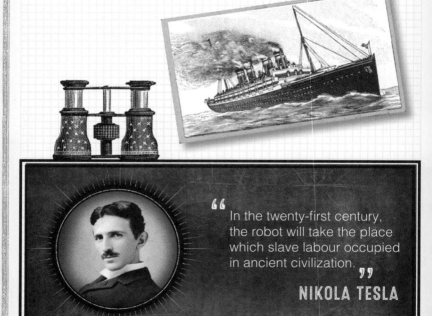

> In the twenty-first century, the robot will take the place which slave labour occupied in ancient civilization.
>
> ## NIKOLA TESLA

SOLUTION ON PAGE 120

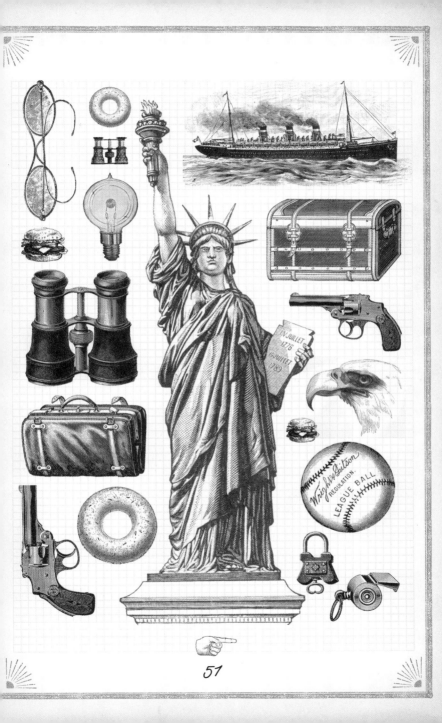

Two of the items above have swapped positions. Can you say which?

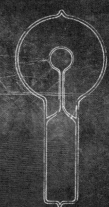

“ We wind a simple ring of iron with coils; we establish the connections to the generator, and with wonder and delight we note the effects of strange forces which we bring into play, which allow us to transform, to transmit and direct energy at will. ”

NIKOLA TESLA

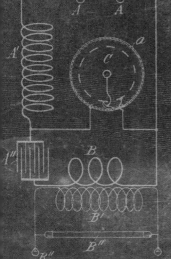

COMPLETE THE GRID IV

What belongs in the empty box?

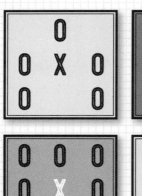
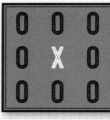

SOLUTION ON PAGE 121

SEQUENCE II

What is the missing number?

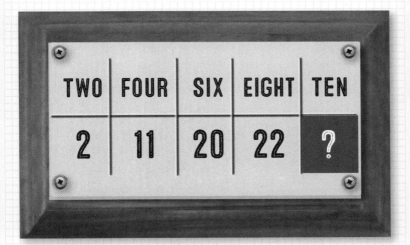

TWO	FOUR	SIX	EIGHT	TEN
2	11	20	22	?

SOLUTION ON PAGE 121

POWER SUPPLY III

1. Place a battery (⚡) in a square adjacent to each lightbulb on the grid.

2. Adjacent squares share a side (north, south, east and west) not just a corner.

3. No battery can be placed adjacent to another battery.

4. The numbers tell you how many batteries must be placed in each row or column.

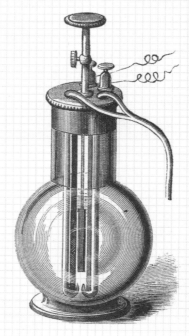

SOLUTION ON PAGE 122

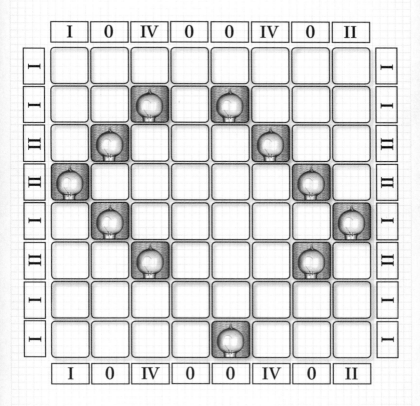

MARATHON

Jack is a gifted athlete who has trained hard for the Olympic marathon. In the last hundred yards he finds the inner strength to increase his pace and overtakes the runner in second place.

But then, with the finishing line just feet away, he is overtaken by two other runners…

What medal will Jack receive?

SOLUTION ON PAGE 123

POWER GRID IV

1. Run a single, unbroken wire around the grid that passes through each of the relays to complete the circuit.

2. The wire must enter and leave each square through the centre of one of its four sides.

3. If the wire enters a black relay, it must immediately turn 90 degrees left or right on that square. It must also pass straight through the square it came from and the square it leads to.

4. If the wire enters a silver relay, it must pass straight through the square. It must also turn left or right in the next and/or preceding square.

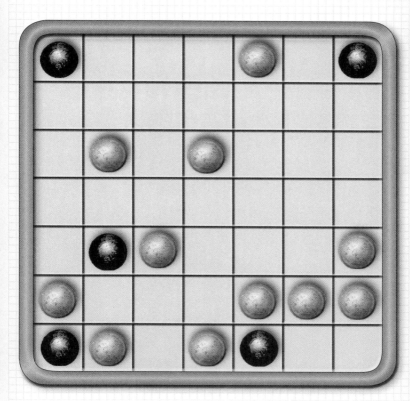

SOLUTION ON PAGE 123

61

POWER SUPPLY IV

1. Place a battery (⚡) in a square adjacent to each lightbulb on the grid.

2. Adjacent squares share a side (north, south, east and west) not just a corner.

3. No battery can be placed adjacent to another battery.

4. The numbers tell you how many batteries must be placed in each row or column.

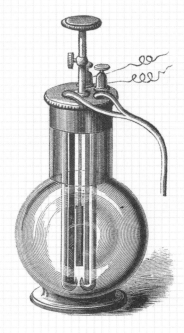

SOLUTION ON PAGE 125

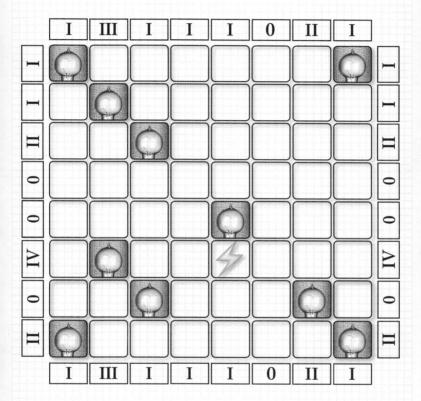

MULTI-DISCIPLINARY

Professor Grohl, Professor Dickinson and Professor Hendrix are all multitalented; each of them specializes in four fields. There are two specialists assigned to each of the six fields listed in the table opposite.

Using your powers of logical deduction can you work out who specializes in what from the statements?

SOLUTION ON PAGE 126

If Grohl specializes in zoology then he also understands psychology

If Grohl specializes in psychology then he doesn't understand chemistry

If Grohl specializes in chemistry then he doesn't understand geology

If Hendrix specializes in mathematics then she doesn't understand zoology

If Hendrix specializes in zoology then she also understands geology

If Hendrix specializes in geology then she also understands chemistry

If Dickinson specializes in chemistry then she also understands geology

If Dickinson specializes in geology then she doesn't understand zoology

If Dickinson specializes in zoology then she doesn't understand mathematics

	GROHL	HENDRIX	DICKINSON
CHEMISTRY			
GEOLOGY			
ZOOLOGY			
MATHEMATICS			
PSYCHOLOGY			
ASTRONOMY			

VALUE SYSTEM III

Work out the value of each component to determine what number replaces the question mark.

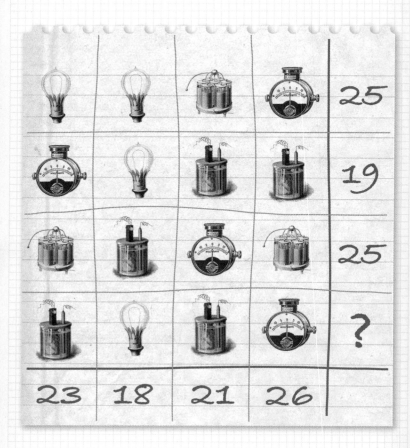

TELEFORCE

Tesla has constructed two prototypes for his "Death Ray" tower.

Tower A can fire a beam of energy five times in five seconds, Tower B can fire ten times in ten seconds.

Assuming that he starts his watch when the first shot is fired, which tower can fire 12 beams in the shorter time?

" There is no memory or retentive faculty based on lasting impression. What we designate as memory is but increased responsiveness to repeated stimuli. "

NIKOLA TESLA

SOLUTION ON PAGE 127

POWER GRID V

1. *Run a single, unbroken wire around the grid that passes through each of the relays to complete the circuit.*

2. *The wire must enter and leave each square through the centre of one of its four sides.*

3. *If the wire enters a black relay, it must immediately turn 90 degrees left or right on that square. It must also pass straight through the square it came from and the square it leads to.*

4. *If the wire enters a silver relay, it must pass straight through the square. It must also turn left or right in the next and/or preceding square.*

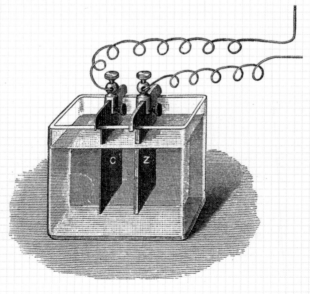

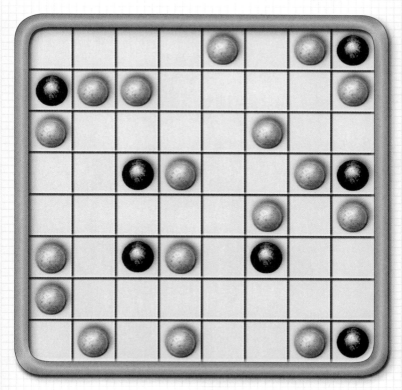

SOLUTION ON PAGE 128

ELECTRIC CITY

The awards for the most Innovative City will soon be announced.
Can you work out the order of the prize winners, the city, the name of its mayor and its unique innovation?

1. The spaceport in Jackson connected Mississippi with the rest of the known universe.

2. Payne, who wasn't Mayor of Seattle, and Mayor Tomlinson, whose city could control its own weather, finished with one prize-winning city between them.

3. The third prize went to Mayor Styles' city which was located on the east coast.

4. The city with the zero gravity sports arena took the second prize; it wasn't Miami.

Prize	City	Mayor	Innovation
First			
Second			
Third			
Fourth			

SOLUTION ON PAGE 128

	Miami	Seattle	Jackson	Boston	Styles	Tomlinson	Horan	Payne	Spaceport	Weather control	Undersea dome	Zero gravity arena
First Prize												
Second Prize												
Third Prize												
Fourth Prize												
Spaceport												
Weather control												
Undersea dome												
Zero gravity arena												
Styles												
Tomlinson												
Horan												
Payne												

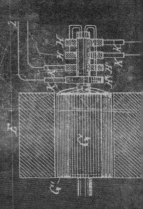

" I do not think there is any thrill that can go through the human heart like that felt by the inventor as he sees some creation of the brain unfolding to success... such emotions make a man forget food, sleep, friends, love, everything. "

NIKOLA TESLA

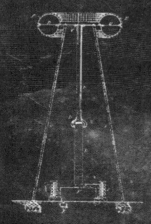

72

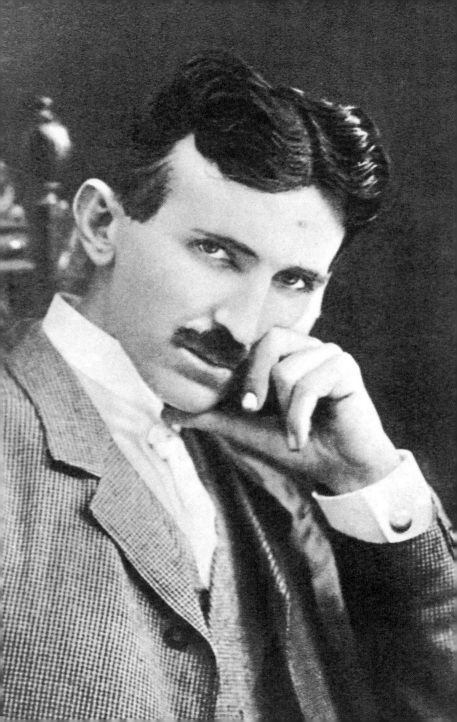

CHAOS

In 1895, while Tesla was still mourning the death of his mother, further disaster struck. A fire tore through his New York workshop leaving all his work in ashes.

On the opposite page you can see a variety of images. Take a couple of minutes to picture them in your mind and then turn over the page…

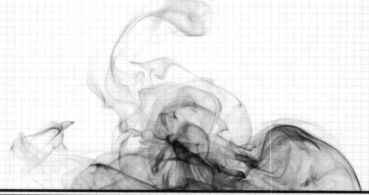

> " Archimedes was my ideal. I admired the works of artists, but to my mind, they were only shadows and semblances. The inventor, I thought, gives to the world creations which are palpable, which live and work. "

NIKOLA TESLA

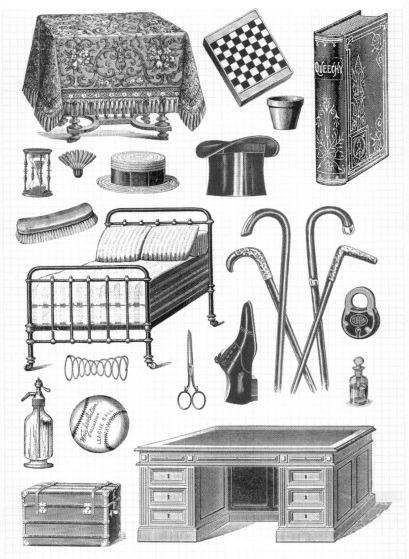

*Write down everything you can remember from the previous page – no **peeking!***

1	
2	
3	
4	
5	
6	
7	
8	
9	
10	
11	
12	
13	
14	
15	
16	
17	
18	
19	
20	

SOLUTION ON PAGE 129

FACING FACTS

Three competitive chemists Alice, Brigitte and Carly have been working on an anti-aging tonic. Each of them takes a vial of their own formula and drinks…

Within a few minutes the face of each scientist has turned an alarming shade of green!

All three burst into fits of laughter at the ridiculous state of the other two.

But Alice stops immediately when she realizes that her own face must have changed colour.

Can you explain how she came to this conclusion?

SOLUTION ON PAGE 129

VALUE SYSTEM IV

Work out the value of each component to determine what number replaces the question mark.

BREAK IN

Some people were envious of Tesla's work. But to what lengths would they go to bring him down?

One night two men broke into Tesla's lab. One took an axe to the door of his workshop and made a quick search of the room before leaving the place in utter chaos.

When Tesla returned to the building, he found his entire life's work in ruins. The two intruders were standing nearby, only feet away from a police officer. Tesla was certain that the men had broken into his lab, but he did not press charges.

Why?

SOLUTION ON PAGE 130

TOWN PLANNING II

Your city is divided into six districts. The mayor has decreed that each district shall have one of each of the following facilities:

 Housing Factory Offices

 School Stadium Park

SOLUTION ON PAGE 131

You must make sure that there is no more than one of each facility in each column and row, and that no facilities of the same type are adjacent to one another.

LIFE FORCE

After losing his life's work, Tesla's life spiralled into madness. He developed an interest in Indian mysticism and became a disciple of the chemist, and mystic, Sir William Crookes and even began using electricity on himself.

On the opposite page you can see a variety of images. Take a couple of minutes to picture them in your mind and then turn over the page…

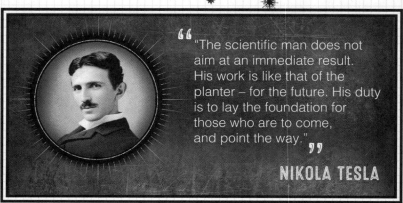

66 "The scientific man does not aim at an immediate result. His work is like that of the planter – for the future. His duty is to lay the foundation for those who are to come, and point the way." 99

NIKOLA TESLA

SOLUTION ON PAGE 132

Two of the items above have swapped positions. Can you say which?

VALUE SYSTEM V

Work out the value of each component to determine what number replaces the question mark.

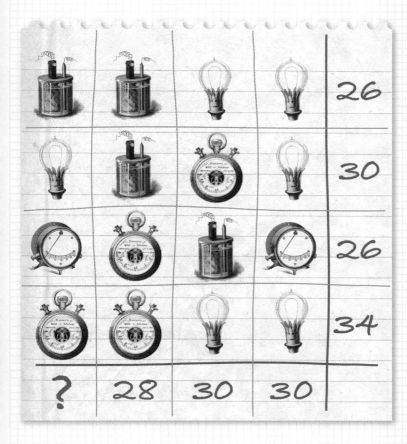

SOLUTION ON PAGE 133

POWER SUPPLY V

1. Place a battery (⚡) in a square adjacent to each lightbulb on the grid.

2. Adjacent squares share a side (north, south, east and west) not just a corner.

3. No battery can be placed adjacent to another battery.

4. The numbers tell you how many batteries must be placed in each row or column.

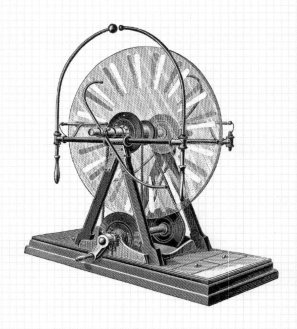

SOLUTION ON PAGE 134

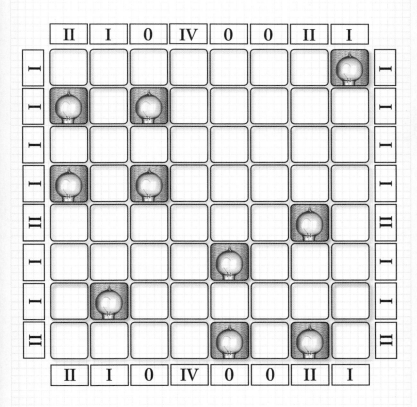

HIDDEN GENIUS

How many great minds do you know?

How many of them can you find in this grid?

N	I	E	T	S	N	E	G	T	T	I	W	A	L	O	A	G	A
O	C	A	O	A	E	K	A	D	I	P	U	I	M	Y	V	O	A
R	I	T	Z	I	C	N	M	I	J	E	H	F	A	G	G	Y	S
A	Y	B	W	D	E	Y	A	W	A	C	E	V	U	S	A	A	R
W	S	A	P	G	E	A	L	S	E	T	K	A	Z	E	L	C	D
D	I	N	A	C	A	O	O	I	A	O	G	A	D	F	I	G	E
A	Q	E	S	A	V	H	L	Z	E	N	E	L	E	A	L	O	T
A	T	C	C	O	B	J	Z	E	E	L	C	Q	S	F	E	E	D
S	R	A	A	K	O	C	A	E	G	T	V	U	Y	A	O	U	A
A	G	Z	L	O	H	H	P	L	W	N	U	O	R	S	O	E	R
V	I	F	M	B	R	A	I	T	C	Q	A	D	Z	I	T	H	D
O	M	E	V	E	T	E	G	O	O	S	X	L	A	I	E	A	Y
S	A	N	H	A	U	D	C	T	L	E	L	O	E	M	N	G	A
E	S	E	T	A	R	C	O	S	Q	I	E	J	A	H	P	E	B
D	S	I	O	Y	E	B	A	I	E	N	B	M	O	A	C	J	I
E	R	T	D	V	L	A	T	R	S	S	A	T	E	S	A	I	L
M	A	R	C	E	A	P	J	A	A	T	N	A	C	X	E	H	M
I	Y	D	E	D	S	H	A	U	T	E	E	V	F	R	A	S	Ö
H	O	I	N	Q	L	C	V	E	A	I	O	B	I	G	K	D	K
C	A	B	G	A	M	U	A	S	N	N	A	O	U	A	E	B	A
R	S	K	A	F	E	A	R	R	E	P	I	E	T	O	X	P	M
A	A	Z	H	I	D	L	Z	N	T	A	D	M	A	A	L	T	S
Y	U	A	S	E	M	A	E	J	A	E	P	A	N	I	L	H	X
I	A	I	C	N	I	V	A	D	O	N	S	O	I	U	R	P	I

SOLUTION ON PAGE 135

HARDWIRE

Tesla has been wiring up his new workshop. He has three identical wires which run from the basement to his lab on the top floor. The wires had been tagged at both ends. Unfortunately, after the wires have been run through the building he finds that the labels (A, B and C) he attached to the top floor wires have fallen off.

He has a machine that will show if a current is passing through a wire but only if both ends of the wire are attached to the machine. How many trips downstairs must he make to determine which wire is which?

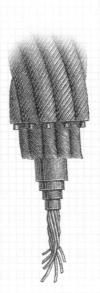

SOLUTION ON PAGE 136

POWER GRID VI

1. *Run a single, unbroken wire around the grid that passes through each of the relays to complete the circuit.*

2. *The wire must enter and leave each square through the centre of one of its four sides.*

3. *If the wire enters a black relay, it must immediately turn 90 degrees left or right on that square. It must also pass straight through the square it came from and the square it leads to.*

4. *If the wire enters a silver relay, it must pass straight through the square. It must also turn left or right in the next and/or preceding square.*

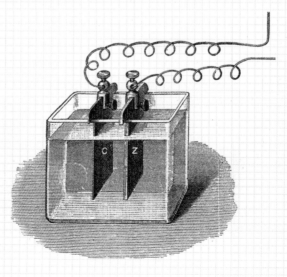

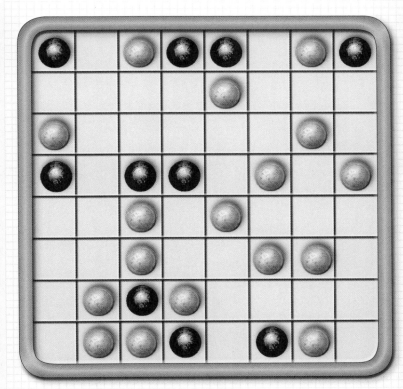

SOLUTION ON PAGE 137

91

VALUE SYSTEM VI

Work out the value of each component to determine what number replaces the question mark.

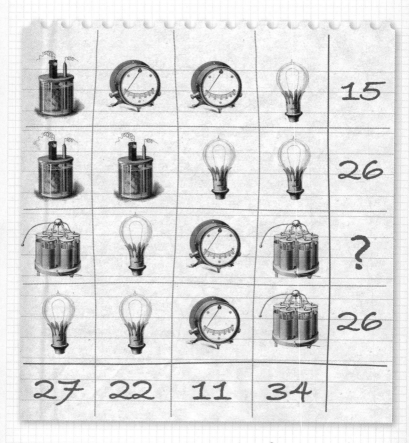

SOLUTION ON PAGE 138

MARK TWAIN

Nikola Tesla was friends with renowned author Mark Twain. Below is a quote from Twain encrypted. Can you decode it?

```
H    T    N    I    N    G
B    H    G    L    N    G
H    U    N    A    N    D
T    T    E    I    I    G
E    H    W    L    E    N
R    T    N    E    E    B
E    E    I    C    F    E
R    D    T    F    T    H
E    I    A    S    T    E
Y    M    L    T    R    G
S    A    E    A    L    L
T    R    O    R    D    I
H    W    R    I    W    H
R    E    A    N    T    T
I    D    H    T    E    O
L    G    O    S    E    R
E    M    T    H    N    A
E    N    E    T    I    E
F    B    R    E    W    C
T    E    E    D    N    F
     H              I
```

SOLUTION ON PAGE 139

93

POWER SUPPLY VI

1. Place a battery (⚡) in a square adjacent to each lightbulb on the grid.

2. Adjacent squares share a side (north, south, east and west) not just a corner.

3. No battery can be placed adjacent to another battery.

4. The numbers tell you how many batteries must be placed in each row or column.

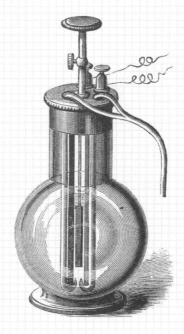

SOLUTION ON PAGE 140

94

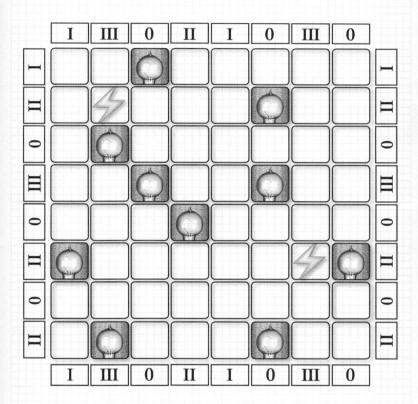

TOWER OF DREAMS

Tesla's new tower was completed. The total value of the project was one million dollars.

The cost of construction was $900,000 more than the cost of the land. So what did Tesla pay for the land?

The real Tesla Tower (Wardenclyffe Tower) was built in 1901. Tesla ultimately intended it to be a means of wireless power transmission but he was unable to find investors and it was abandoned in 1906.

SOLUTION ON PAGE 141

SCIENCE CONFERENCE

A group of eminent scientists meet in Vienna.

All but two of them are biologists.

All but two of them are chemists.

All but two of them are physicists.

How many scientists attend the conference?

SOLUTION ON PAGE 142

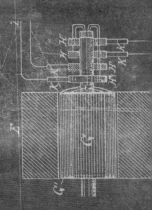

SOLUTIONS

BORN IN A STORM

All of the months have 28 days (including the ones with 30 and 31 days).

COMPLETE THE GRID I

Each row and column contains two silver squares
and a total of five rivets.

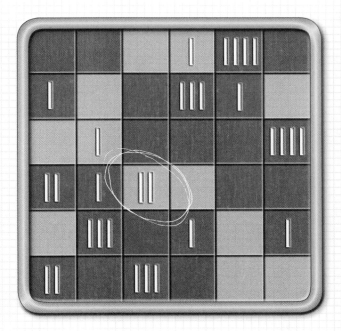

FAITH, HOPE AND CLARITY

SEQUENCE I

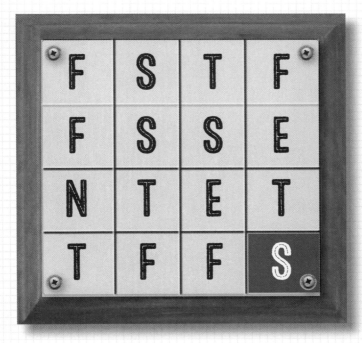

F	S	T	F
F	S	S	E
N	T	E	T
T	F	F	S

First	Second	Third	Fourth
Fifth	Sixth	Seventh	Eighth
Ninth	Tenth	Eleventh	Twelfth
Thirteenth	Fourteenth	Fifteenth	Sixteenth

STONE AGE PIONEERS

	Invention	Inspiration	Reward
Zog	Fire	Hunting	Worshipped
Ugg	Wheel	Mushrooms	Banished
Stig	Plough	Sabre-tooth tiger	Monument
Nigel	Bow	Thunderstorm	Promoted to chief

POWER GRID I

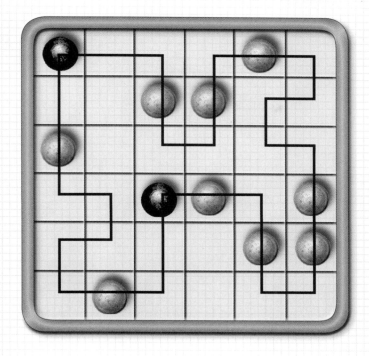

VISIONS

WATERY GRAVE

The water in the three rooms was in different states: liquid, solid and gas. So the man in contact with the ice died of hypothermia and/or suffocation, and the one in the room full of steam perished from burns and dehydration.

PATTERN RECOGNITION

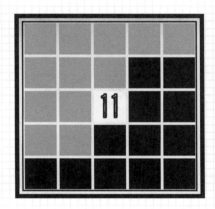

A. The shape rotates counter-clockwise and the numbers increase by +1, +2, +3, +4 etc.

COMPLETE THE GRID II

Each row and column contains two black squares and three electrical discharges, two domes and one switch.

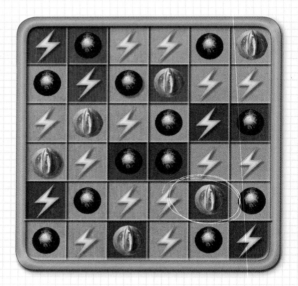

FAMILIARITY

Sir Avery had three daughters: identical triplets, one of whom was raised by his ex-wife. Clara and Betty recognized the familiar features of their long-lost sister and were upset that their portion of the will would have to be split three ways.

VALUE SYSTEM I

The missing number is 12.

 5 4 2 3

IT'S ALIVE!

Professor	Location	Golem	Outcome
Van der Volt	New York	Bob	Bloody rampage
Bankenstein	Paris	Jerry	Got married
Knutz	Berlin	Ron	National hero
Phreekdoubt	London	Phil	Therapy

POWER SUPPLY I

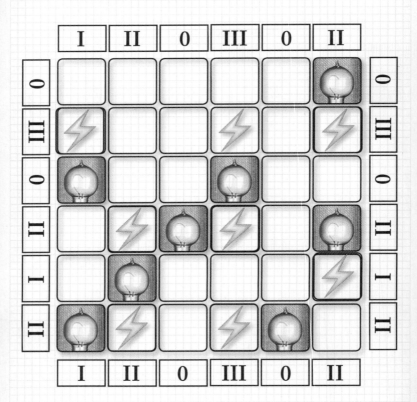

VALUE SYSTEM II

The missing number is 13.

 7 1 3 5

> " Life is and will ever remain an equation incapable of solution, but it contains certain known factors. "
>
> ## NIKOLA TESLA

TOWN PLANNING I

POWER GRID II

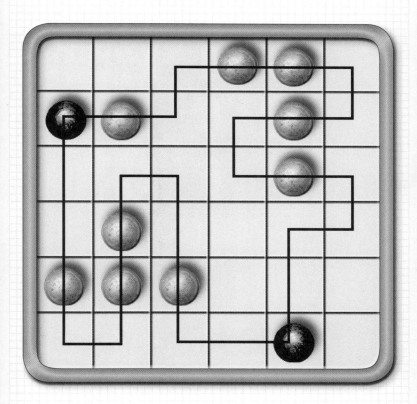

COMPLETE THE GRID III

FREQUENCY

1: Isaac Newton
2: Albert Einstein
3: Michael Faraday
4: Nikola Tesla

POWER SUPPLY II

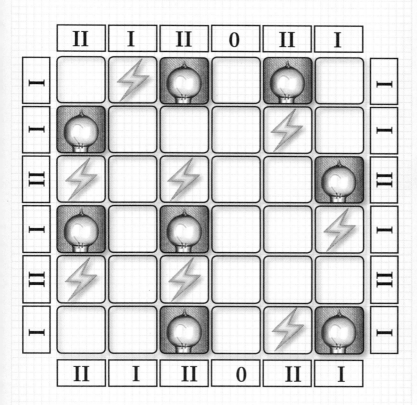

SCIENCE VS CATASTROPHE

Professor	Field	Catastrophe	Solution
Dick Dorkins	Astrophysics	Global flood	Move to Mars
Ty Neilson	Marine Biology	Meteor strike	Live underground
Harry Stottle	Geology	Alien invasion	Genetic mutation
Gary Leo	Paleontology	Ice Age	Robot servants

POWER GRID III

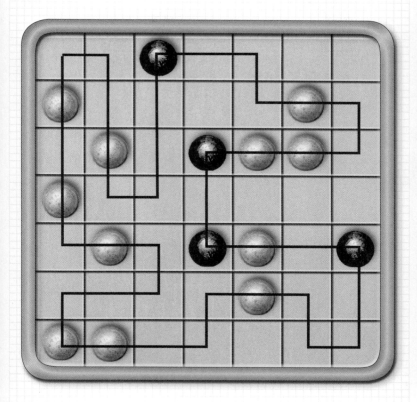

RESEARCH

Only accountants can claim to be statisticians because real statisticians have to pretend to be something else and biochemists cannot lie. So Team 2 is Alpha Team.

Alpha (2)
6 accountants changing the truth so they now become
6 statisticians

The biochemists cannot pretend to be anything other than what they are and we know that some must be present in Charlie Team, which means Charlie Team is Team 1.

Charlie (1)
2 biochemists truthfully claiming to be biochemists
2 statisticians falsely claiming to be biochemists
2 accountants changing the truth so they now
become biochemists

So that leaves us with Bravo Team as Team 3 which must consist of statisticians and accountants.

Bravo (3)
3 statisticians falsely claiming to be accountants
3 accountants truthfully claiming to be accountants

So 11 lying statisticians are sent home!

BAGELS

First determine how many bagels the seller started with by working backwards (adding two bagels and doubling the result) for each gang.

After the third gang	1 bagel	+2 x2 = 6 bagels
After the second gang	6 bagels	+2 x2 = 16 bagels
After the first gang	16 bagels	+2 x2 = 36 bagels

Multiplying the 36 bagels by $0.02 gives $0.72 which the seller pays each day.

So the bagel seller makes a daily profit (from his single bagel sale at $1.50) of $0.78, just enough to buy his next consignment and pocketing a meagre six cents.

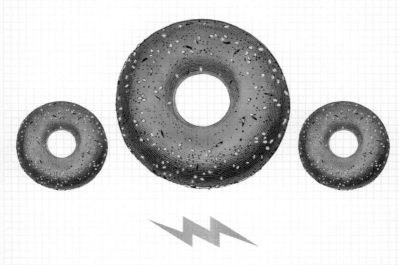

NEW WORLD

COMPLETE THE GRID IV

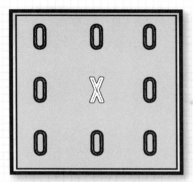

SEQUENCE II

101. The numbers on the bottom row are the Base 3 (ternary) equivalents of the decimal numbers on the top row.

One	Two	Three	Four	Five
1	2	10	11	12
Six	Seven	Eight	Nine	Ten
20	21	22	100	**101**

POWER SUPPLY III

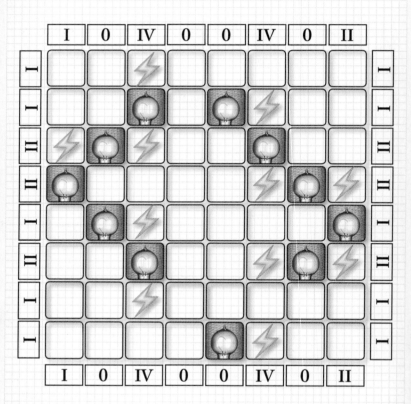

MARATHON

None. You might have been tempted to say 'bronze' if you made the mistake of thinking that overtaking the second place runner would put Jack in first place; in fact Jack would replace that runner in second place and would pushed back to forth by the other two runners.

POWER GRID IV

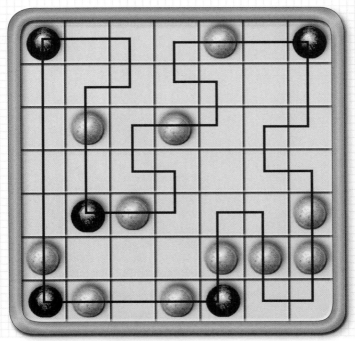

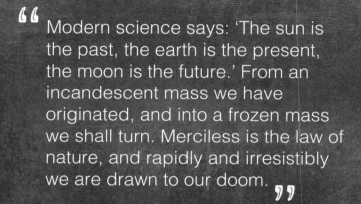

Modern science says: 'The sun is the past, the earth is the present, the moon is the future.' From an incandescent mass we have originated, and into a frozen mass we shall turn. Merciless is the law of nature, and rapidly and irresistibly we are drawn to our doom.

NIKOLA TESLA

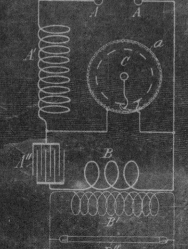

POWER SUPPLY IV

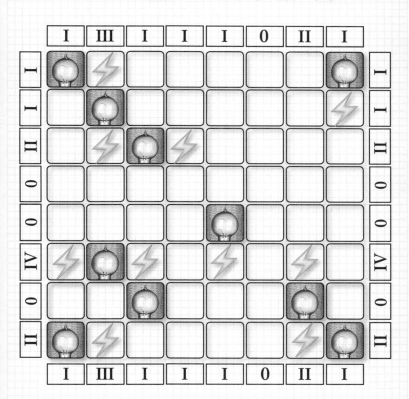

MULTI-DISCIPLINARY

	GROHL	HENDRIX	DICKINSON
CHEMISTRY		✓	✓
GEOLOGY	✓	✓	
ZOOLOGY	✓		✓
MATHEMATICS	✓	✓	
PSYCHOLOGY	✓		✓
ASTRONOMY		✓	✓

VALUE SYSTEM III

The missing number is 19.

 8 3 5 7

TELEFORCE

Tower B has the faster rate of fire. The important factor here is the interval between firings.

Tower A: There are 4 intervals between the first and fifth shot; dividing intervals by the time taken gives 1.25 seconds per interval.

Tower B: There are 9 intervals between the first and tenth shot; dividing intervals by the time taken gives 1.11 seconds per interval.

Tower A will take 13.75 seconds to fire 12 shots (11 intervals) whereas Tower B will take 12.21 seconds.

POWER GRID V

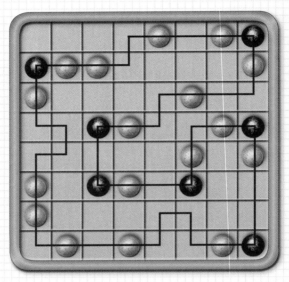

ELECTRIC CITY

Prize	City	Mayor	Innovation
First	Jackson	Horan	Spaceport
Second	Boston	Payne	Zero G arena
Third	Miami	Styles	Undersea dome
Fourth	Seattle	Tomlinson	Weather control

CHAOS

TABLE AND CLOTH	TOP HAT	PADLOCK
GAMES BOARD	CLOTHES BRUSH	TINCTURE BOTTLE
FLOWER POT	BED	SODA SYPHON
BOOK	SPRING	BASEBALL
HOURGLASS	SCISSORS	CHEST
SHUTTLECOCK	SHOE	DESK
BOATER HAT	WALKING CANES	

Alice concludes that everyone was laughing because, like her, they initially believed they hadn't been affected. If Bertha believed this and saw that Alice's face was unaffected, Carly's laughter would make no sense; Bertha would then conclude that Carly was laughing at her and she would stop laughing herself. Since Bertha hadn't stopped laughing she must have concluded that Carly is laughing at Alice.

VALUE SYSTEM IV

The missing number is 26.

 4 7 9 5

BREAK IN

The two men were firefighters. Sadly, a fire really did destroy Tesla's Fifth Avenue laboratory in 1895.

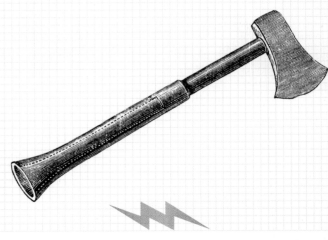

TOWN PLANNING II

LIFE FORCE

VALUE SYSTEM V

The missing number is 28.

 6   5   8   9

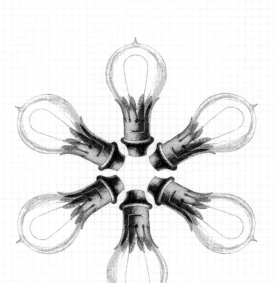

POWER SUPPLY V

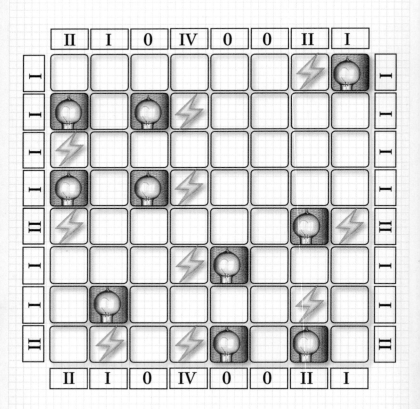

HIDDEN GENIUS

There are 14 great thinkers in the grid:

N	I	E	T	S	N	E	G	T	T	I	W	A	L	O	A	G	A
O	C	A	O	A	E	K	A	D	I	P	U	I	M	Y	V	O	A
R	I	T	Z	I	C	N	M	I	J	E	H	F	A	G	G	Y	S
A	Y	B	W	D	E	Y	A	W	A	C	E	V	U	S	A	A	R
W	S	A	P	G	E	A	L	S	E	T	K	A	Z	E	L	C	D
D	I	N	A	C	A	O	O	I	A	O	G	A	D	F	I	G	E
A	Q	E	S	A	V	H	L	Z	E	N	E	L	E	A	L	O	T
A	T	C	C	O	B	J	Z	E	E	L	C	Q	S	F	E	E	D
S	R	A	A	K	O	C	A	E	G	T	V	U	Y	A	O	U	A
A	G	Z	L	O	H	H	P	L	W	N	U	O	R	S	O	E	R
V	I	F	M	B	R	A	I	T	C	Q	A	D	Z	I	T	H	D
O	M	E	V	E	T	E	G	O	O	S	X	L	A	I	E	A	Y
S	A	N	H	A	U	D	C	T	L	E	L	O	E	M	N	G	A
E	S	E	T	A	R	C	O	S	Q	I	E	J	A	H	P	E	B
D	S	I	O	Y	E	B	A	I	E	N	B	M	O	A	C	J	I
E	R	T	D	V	L	A	T	R	S	S	A	T	E	S	A	I	L
M	A	R	C	E	A	P	J	A	A	T	N	A	C	X	E	H	M
I	Y	D	E	D	S	H	A	U	T	E	E	V	F	R	A	S	O
H	O	I	N	Q	L	C	V	E	A	I	O	B	I	G	K	D	K
C	A	B	G	A	M	U	A	S	N	N	A	O	U	A	E	B	A
R	S	K	A	F	E	A	R	R	E	P	I	E	T	O	X	P	M
A	A	Z	H	I	D	L	Z	N	T	A	D	M	A	A	L	T	S
Y	U	A	S	E	M	A	E	J	A	E	P	A	N	I	L	H	X
I	A	I	C	N	I	V	A	D	O	N	S	O	I	U	R	P	I

(Ludwig) WITTGENSTEIN, (Blaise) PASCAL, GALILEO,
(Nikola) TESLA, (Niels) BOHR, MICHELANGELO,
ARCHIMEDES, (Marie) CURIE, (Albert) EINSTEIN,
ARISTOTLE, (René) DESCARTES, SOCRATES,
PLATO, (Leonardo) DAVINCI

HARDWIRE

Tesla must make a minimum of two trips downstairs. Tesla goes down to the basement where the three wires are labelled. He connects wire A to wire B then goes back upstairs. He attaches pairs of wires to his machine (there are three possible combinations) until he finds the one that makes a circuit. The other wire is therefore 'C' so he attaches the appropriate label to it. Then he connects the newly labelled 'C' wire to one of the other wires which he labels 'A' and the remaining wire 'B'.

Going back to the basement he attaches wire 'A' to wire 'C'. If it shows a current, all the wires are correct. Otherwise he swaps over the labels 'A' and 'B', and the job is good.

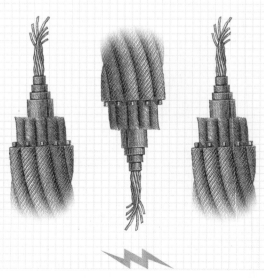

POWER GRID VI

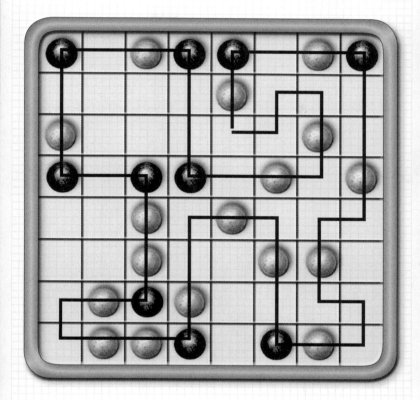

VALUE SYSTEM X

The missing number is 27.

 1 5 8 9

> " As in nature, all is ebb and tide, all is wave motion, so it seems that in all branches of industry, alternating currents – electric wave motion – will have the sway. "
>
> **NIKOLA TESLA**

MARK TWAIN

The quote has been stripped of spaces and punctuation and broken into blocks of six letters, then the blocks have been reordered back to front.

"The difference between the almost right word and the right word is really a large matter - it's the difference between the lightning-bug and the lightning"

POWER SUPPLY VI

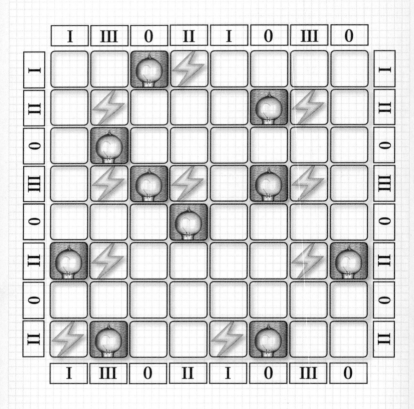

140

TOWER OF DREAMS

If you don't think about the question properly, you might answer $100,000, but that would take the cost of construction alone up to $1,000,000, making the total cost $1,100,000.

The correct answer is $50,000.

SCIENCE CONFERENCE

Just three scientists.

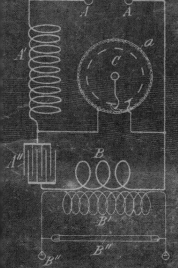

"That is the trouble with many inventors; they lack patience. They lack the willingness to work a thing out slowly and clearly and sharply in their mind, so that they can actually 'feel it work.' They want to try their first idea right off; and the result is they use up lots of money and lots of good material, only to find eventually that they are working in the wrong direction. We all make mistakes, and it is better to make them before we begin."

NIKOLA TESLA

143

PUZZLE NOTES